The Secret Beach

Jane Rollason

Series Editor: Rob Waring

HEINLE
CENGAGE Learning™

Australia • Brazil • Japan • Korea • Mexico • Singapore • Spain • United Kingdom • United States

HEINLE
CENGAGE Learning™

Page Turners Reading Library
The Secret Beach
Jane Rollason

Publisher: Andrew Robinson
Executive Editor: Sean Bermingham
Senior Development Editor:
Derek Mackrell
Assistant Editors:
Claire Tan, Sarah Tan
Story Editor: Julian Thomlinson
Series Development Editor:
Sue Leather
Director of Global Marketing:
Ian Martin
Content Project Manager:
Tan Jin Hock
Print Buyer:
Susan Spencer
Layout Design and Illustrations:
Redbean Design Pte Ltd
Cover Illustration: Eric Foenander

Photo Credits:
45 mushakesa/iStockphoto,
56 Deejpilot/iStockphoto,
57 duncan1890/iStockphoto,
59 jeannehatch/iStockphoto,
60 sunny-k/iStockphoto

ISBN-13: 978-1-4240-1842-0

ISBN-10: 1-4240-1842-0

Heinle
20 Channel Center Street
Boston, Massachusetts 02210
USA

Cengage Learning is a leading provider of customized learning solutions with office locations around the globe, including Singapore, the United Kingdom, Australia, Mexico, Brazil, and Japan. Locate your local office at:
international.cengage.com/region

Cengage Learning products are represented in Canada by Nelson Education, Ltd.

Visit Heinle online at **elt.heinle.com**

Visit our corporate website at
www.cengage.com

Printed in the United States of America
3 4 5 6 7 – 14

Contents

People in the story

Lucas Gray
a nineteen-year-old surfer
who lives in Cornwall

Ella Croft
a nineteen-year-old law student
who lives in London

Jerry Maxwell
Ella's boyfriend, who is also a
law student in London

The story is set in Cornwall, in the southwest of England.

Chapter 1

City boys

Lucas watched the wave and waited. His heart beat fast. This was a perfect wave. The blue wall of water began to move his surfboard. He stood up and rode along the top of the wave. He turned and his board cut through the side of the wave. He lived for these moments. He felt the power of the sea. He was part of it.

Later, Lucas pulled his board out of the water. He heard voices and looked up at the top of the cliff. It was Max. He was a local boy and he lived near Lucas.

"Hi, Max," shouted Lucas. Max looked down at him but he didn't answer. Then a stranger appeared behind him. He looked about Lucas's age, with short black hair. Max showed him the way down to the beach.

The stranger gave Max some money. Lucas watched as Max took the money and walked away.

There wasn't only one stranger. There were seven of them. They started to come down the cliff. They all carried surfboards.

To Lucas, they looked like rich city kids. They put their bags in the middle of the beach.

"This is better," said the boy with black hair. "I like it here. The surfing looks good here." He didn't look at Lucas, but the girls said hello. Three of the strangers took their boards into the sea. Lucas sat on a rock and watched.

The new surfers tried to ride a big wave. The sea pushed them toward the rocks at the side of the beach. They all fell off their boards. The boy with black hair hit the rocks. The others ran down to the sea. The boy caught the board and swam to the beach.

"Are you okay, Jerry?" called one of the girls.

"No," shouted Jerry. "And I broke my board."

"Maybe it's too difficult here," said the girl.

"Difficult?" said Jerry. He came out of the water. "Give me your board, Ella. I'm going out again." He looked angrily at Lucas.

Jerry fell off again, but he didn't break the board this time. The group all took their boards into the water, except the girl called Ella. Lucas looked across at her. She was smiling and laughing at her friends. She was lovely. Suddenly she looked at Lucas and their eyes met. She smiled at him, and he felt on fire inside.

Lucas went into the water again. He swam out to the best place and waited. He caught a wave and surfed in beautifully. Was the girl watching him?

He went out again, and looked around. The boy with black hair—Jerry—was behind him. They waited for a good wave. When it came, Lucas picked up the wave perfectly. He jumped off when he came close to the rocks. Suddenly something hit him. Jerry was in the water right next to him.

"Hey!" cried Jerry. "Look out!" Both boys swam to the beach.

"Are you okay?" asked Lucas. He wasn't smiling. "What happened?"

"You only surfed to the rocks," said Jerry. He wasn't smiling either. "I was going all the way in."

"Why didn't you wait for the next wave?" asked Lucas.

"That was the perfect wave," Jerry replied.

"That was dangerous surfing," said Lucas.

"I like dangerous surfing," said Jerry.

"You don't know the waves and the rocks here. You should go to the town beach for the big waves," said Lucas.

"I've surfed bigger waves on smaller beaches," said Jerry.

"We get very big waves here sometimes—'Titans,' we call them. You shouldn't try those," said Lucas.

"Just watch me," said Jerry.

Lucas wasn't going to win any arguments with this guy. He decided to leave, and walked across the warm sand toward the cliff. The girl was still sitting on the sand and she smiled at him. Suddenly he wasn't angry anymore.

"Enjoy the sun," he said.

"Thanks," she said. "What happened out there?"

"Your friend was too close to me," said Lucas. "That's not a good idea here."

"Are you leaving because of that?" the girl asked. She looked worried.

"No, I have to get back to town," said Lucas.

"As long as you're okay," she said.

"Me? I'm fine. I live here. That happens all the time," said Lucas.

She smiled and stood up. And then she walked down to the water.

Lucas climbed to the top of the cliff and put his board on top of his old blue car. He usually thought about the waves on the drive back to town. Today he thought about the sun on the girl's hair and her beautiful smile. How could he get to see her again?

Chapter 2

The lesson

Lucas was at the Surf School on the town beach. He had to give a lesson to a beginner at two thirty and then to a group of teenagers at four thirty.

He looked at his watch. Two twenty-five.

Max walked by.

"Max, hey," called Lucas. "What were you thinking? Seven city kids on Karrek Beach?"

"Hi, Lucas," said Max. "You know what? They paid me a lot of money."

"What about Five Points Beach or Morvoren? Why did you bring them to our beach?"

"They wanted great surfing and no people, Lucas. There's only one beach that's like that. And anyone can find Karrek Beach on the Internet. Don't give me a hard time."

Max walked on.

"Excuse me," said a voice behind Lucas. "I've got a lesson with . . . umm . . . Lucas, is it?"

Lucas turned.

"I'm Lucas," he said. "Oh . . . hi!"

"Hello again," she smiled. "My name's Ella. I loved that little beach this morning."

There was her lovely smile again. Her brown eyes were half closed in the sun.

"Yeah," he said. "Karrek Beach—that little beach is called Karrek—it's a local secret!"

"Oh no!" she laughed. "It *was* a local secret."

Lucas laughed, too.

"Okay, ready? Let's go."

They walked toward the sea.

"Have you surfed much?" Lucas asked.

"I started a few weeks ago."

"How about your friends?"

"Jerry—that's my boyfriend—he and his friends go surfing most weekends; they go to different beaches. Sometimes they go down to France or Spain."

"That's expensive!" said Lucas.

"Oh, you know, they have rich parents," said Ella. "We're at university in London together. Jerry asked me down here. I want lessons because I want to surf with the boys. They talk about 'dropping in' and 'cutbacks' all the time—I don't know what they mean!"

"Okay," said Lucas. "Well, when you 'drop in,' that means you catch a wave that another surfer is riding—that's a bad thing to do."

"And a cutback?"

"That's when you jump and turn back toward the wave; it gets you closer to the power of the wave."

"Is that it?" she laughed. "They make it sound much more difficult."

After the lesson, they had coffee at a beach café. Lucas looked at Ella. She was strong and tall and, well, lovely.

"You're a great surfer," he said. "You don't look like a beginner."

"Thanks," she said and smiled.

"Once people try it, they really love it."

"Yeah, I want to be really good," said Ella. "I do a lot of dancing. I guess that helps."

"Surfing is like dancing on the waves," said Lucas.

"I watched you at your little beach," she said. "You looked amazing! You weren't very happy when we arrived though."

"For some of us, this beach is our life," he said. He drew pictures in the sand with his feet.

"Some of our friends went away to university or to get big city jobs. We didn't do that. We stayed here. Maybe we feel like it's our place."

"You don't want weekend visitors on your secret beach?" asked Ella.

"No, I don't mean that."

"But you'd like a bit more respect," she said.

"Maybe that's it," said Lucas.

"I know what you mean," said Ella. "You know the sea better than anyone. People from outside need to understand that."

Lucas looked back up the beach. A group of young teenagers were standing at the Surf School.

"My next lesson, I think," he said.

"Oh, right," said Ella happily. "I must get back to my friends!"

They walked back up the beach, carrying their boards. They walked close, and their arms suddenly touched. Fire ran through Lucas's body. He really liked this girl. But although she was very friendly, she didn't seem interested in him. Back at the Surf School, Ella paid for her lesson.

"Perhaps I'll see you again?" Lucas asked.

"See me . . . ?" Ella sounded surprised.

"For another lesson, I mean," he said quickly.

"Oh yeah, perhaps," she said. "Bye."

She walked toward the car park. She turned for a moment and looked at the sea. Lucas was watching her. He saw her smile and laugh. Was she smiling at him? But then he saw her phone in her hand. She was already back in her world.

Chapter 3

Local boys

A week later, Lucas went to Karrek Beach early in the morning. He parked his car above the beach. He jumped out and took his bag from the back seat.

Some of his friends were surfing already.

"Hi, Lucas," called one of them. "We heard about your visitors last weekend."

"Yeah," Lucas shouted back. "They didn't have a great time. I don't think we'll see them again."

The waves were good. Lucas and his friends did difficult moves on their boards.

"Uh-oh!" said one of the boys. "Here comes trouble!"

Lucas looked up. The city boys were back. There were only three of them this time. Lucas said hello to Jerry.

"Hi," said Jerry. "It's busy today."

"Yeah," said one of Lucas's friends. "Very busy."

"Any of your big waves today, do you think?" Jerry asked Lucas.

"You mean Titans? They only come two or three times a year," said Lucas.

"Only this guy can surf Titans," said one of Lucas's friends, putting his arm around Lucas. "He's the best. There's no one like him."

The local boys picked up their boards and swam out. There were lines of waves out on the sea. Each boy took a wave. One after another, they stood up on their boards and rode in. They jumped into the water before they got to the rocks. Lucas came out of the water and sat on a rock. He looked up to the top of the cliff again. He was looking for Ella, but she wasn't there.

Jerry and his friends swam out, but they weren't in a good place to catch a wave. The local boys followed them and waited in a line again.

Lucas looked at his watch. He picked up his board and walked toward the cliff. But then he heard shouts from the sea. He looked back. Jerry and one of the local boys were standing in the water. They were ready to fight.

Lucas ran back, and pulled his friend away.

"Hey!" shouted Lucas. "Let's not get angry here."

"Are we in your way? I'm very sorry," said Jerry. "But it doesn't say 'Locals only' at the top of the cliff. And we're not going anywhere."

"Yeah, the beach is open," said Lucas's friend. "But this is our beach—we come here every day. City people can use the town beach."

"Come on, guys," said Lucas to his friends. "The waves are finished anyway."

Lucas led his friends off Karrek Beach and back to town.

Chapter 4

Trouble

It was wet and windy the next Sunday. Lucas and some of his friends arrived at Karrek Beach.

"Look at that," laughed one of them. It was an old piece of board with some writing on it. "Locals only," it said.

"Who put that there?" said Lucas.

"I don't know," said one of his friends.

"It's not very friendly," said Lucas.

"Who wants to be friends?" laughed his friend.

There were no other people on the beach, and the sea hit the rocks loudly. They went out into the water and they felt its power.

The wind pushed dark gray clouds across the light gray sky.

Later, more of their friends arrived.

"Have you seen our city friends today?" one of them asked.

"No, not yet," said Lucas.

"We'll be ready for them."

"The girls seem nice," said Lucas.

"Yeah," laughed the boys, "very nice!"

The waves were good. The boys flew past each other on their boards.

Later, they heard the sound of fast cars with big engines. The local boys all looked up at the cliff.

The city kids looked down from the top of the cliff. This time they were all there. Ella was there. Jerry laughed at the "Locals only" sign, and they came down to the beach. Ella was nearly at the bottom when she suddenly fell.

"Ow!" she cried. "My foot." Lucas wanted to run over, but there were six people around her. Two of the boys carried her onto the beach. Lucas could see Jerry's face. He wasn't happy.

They all looked at Ella's foot. One girl cleaned it with water and put something round it. Then they got ready for surfing. Ella stayed at the top of the beach. The others went down to the water. There was more blue in the sky now, and the sun came out for a moment.

"I'll see if she's okay," Lucas said to one of his friends. "I know her."

"Hey, are you making friends with the city girls?" smiled his friend. "You didn't tell me!"

"I gave her a lesson last week, that's all. Let's watch our boys," said Lucas. "We don't want any trouble."

Lucas walked across the sand. "Hi," he said. "How's your foot? Can I see?"

Ella held her foot out.

"What a stupid thing to do," she said. "How will I get back up?"

"The cut's not bad, but there's some dirt in it," said Lucas. "I've got some things in my car. I'll get them."

He came back quickly with an orange sports bag. He took out bandages, a fishing knife, and a bottle of water. He cleaned her foot.

"Ow!" cried Ella.

"Sorry," said Lucas.

"What's the knife for? I'm afraid," she said and smiled.

"I'm going to cut the bandage with it," he laughed. "That's all."

"Aren't you surfing today?" she asked.

"It's busy out there," he said. "You didn't come last weekend . . ."

"Oh, did you notice?" she asked, looking at him with interest. "Wasn't there some trouble . . . ?"

"Yeah, a bit. I guess we don't like sharing the best waves!" he said.

"I'm sorry we're here again, then," said Ella. She was smiling but she sounded a bit angry.

"I'm not," Lucas replied, and he put the bandage around her foot.

"Oh . . . ow!"

"Sorry!" he said.

Lucas and Ella looked out to sea. A big wave was coming, and one of the local boys got into position. Jerry dropped into the wave behind him. He was too close, and Lucas's friend suddenly fell off his board. Jerry surfed past and into the beach.

Jerry walked up the sand toward Ella and Lucas.

"Did something happen out there?" asked Lucas.

Jerry didn't answer Lucas. He spoke to Ella.

"How's your foot? And who's your friend?"

"This is Lucas. He cleaned the cut for me and . . ."

"Yeah, thanks, Lucas," said Jerry, without looking at him. "We surfed well out there," he said to Ella. "These local boys can't have all the best waves."

"I'm sure there's room for everyone," said Ella.

Jerry didn't answer. Lucas put his knife and bandages back in his bag. He looked up. Jerry was watching him.

Then Jerry turned back to Ella.

"Let's find a real doctor," he said to her smiling. "And then we'll get some lunch."

"Lucas did a good job. It's fine now."

"Come on," said Jerry. "I'll help you up the cliff."

Ella put her arm around Jerry.

"Shall I take your other arm?" asked Lucas.

"I think we're okay," said Jerry.

"Fine," said Lucas angrily.

"Thanks, Lucas," Ella said. "You were very kind."

Lucas climbed quickly back up the cliff and got into his old blue car. On the way back to town, the car began to lose power. It didn't smell great, either. He stopped at the side of the road. One of his friends, Jack, stopped behind him and together they looked at the engine.

"Why does it have to break down now?" Lucas shouted. "I'm starting work at the restaurant in an hour."

"Because it's very, very old, Lucas," said Jack. "Look at it!"

"OK, I know," said Lucas. "Let's try and start it one more time."

They heard Jerry's new red sports car before they saw it. The car slowed down and stopped next to them.

"Need any help?" called Jerry, a smile on his face.

"I think we're okay, thanks," replied Lucas. He turned his back to hide his face.

Jerry drove off fast. Lucas hit the top of his car hard with his hand.

Chapter 5

A walk under the moon

"Table 9, Lucas," called George, the manager at the Tube restaurant, "then take ten minutes, okay?" Lucas went over to Table 9. They paid and left. Lucas cleared the table and went back into the kitchen.

"Hey, Lucas," said one of the other waiters. "You want to go out later?"

"I can't—no money. I'm saving for a new car; mine's going to die any day now."

"Lucas," shouted the manager. "New group at Table 9."

Lucas looked at Table 9.

"Oh no!" he thought, and then took some menus over.

"Well, look!" said Jerry. "It's our beach doctor."

"Jerry, please!" said Ella. "Hi, Lucas."

"Hi," said Lucas. "What can I get you?"

"Steak for me," said Jerry.

Later, Jerry called Lucas over. He showed him his steak. "Can't you cook a steak down here?"

Ella looked unhappy.

Lucas took the steak back to the kitchen.

"I hear there's a surfing competition in town next month," Jerry said to Lucas, when he came back with another steak. "Will you enter?"

"Yeah," said Lucas. "Probably."

"Then we can see who surfs better—you or me!" said Jerry.

"Excuse me," said Lucas, "I've got work to do."

Table 9 talked and laughed very loudly. The people at other tables looked at them angrily.

They finished their main course, and Lucas came back with the menus. Ella got up.

"I'm really tired," she said. "I think I'll go back to the hotel. Sorry, guys. See you later."

She smiled at Lucas and left.

"What's wrong with those boys?" the manager asked Lucas in the kitchen.

"Oh, there was some trouble with them on Karrek Beach today," Lucas explained.

Jerry and his friends paid and went off to a club in the town.

The restaurant closed soon after. It was a lovely clear night, and Lucas decided to walk home along the beach. There was a big moon in the sky.

"Lucas." He turned. It was Ella. "I waited for you. I wanted to say sorry," she said. "My friends—they were childish. I'm sorry."

"Hey, it's nothing," said Lucas. "It gets much worse in the summer."

"You're so nice," she said.

"I don't think so. We must seem very unfriendly."

Ella laughed. "Well, there is a beach war on!"

They walked down to the sea.

"Let's make a fire," said Lucas. When the fire was going, they sat close to it.

"I'm with them all the time," said Ella after a few minutes. "My friends, I mean. We're law students. We think we're great, I suppose. I don't spend much time with normal people."

"You want 'normal'? Why don't you come down and spend a weekend with me?" said Lucas.

Ella didn't answer.

"Jerry is going to be an amazing lawyer," she said. "He's really quick and clever. When someone is really good at something, I like that." She laughed. "Like you on your surfboard."

"I guess a lawyer is better than a surfer any day," said Lucas.

"I'm not so sure," said Ella quietly. "He's quite dangerous, and that's exciting, but . . . like this evening . . . sometimes he's really not very nice. And then I don't want to be with him anymore."

The sea was quiet under the moon.

"Have you always lived here?" Ella asked.

"Yes," he said looking toward the dark town behind them. "I've always been on boats and on the sea. I worked for my dad in the school holidays. He has a boat business. He's working over in Maui in Hawaii right now. He takes surfers out to the big waves."

"Wow! Why don't you go and work for him?"

"Maybe I will. But that's my dad's life. I love the sea here; my friends are here; my life's here. I know this sea."

"I love the sea too," said Ella. "My parents always took us sailing in the holidays."

"Now, let me guess. You lived in the country and went to an expensive school. Now you live in your parents' large flat in an expensive part of London. Am I close?"

"Good try, Lucas, but wrong. I went to a normal school in London. And I have a very small room in a big house with lots of other students . . . I work four evenings a week to pay for it . . ."

". . . and you have a very beautiful smile," said Lucas.

"I think I'll go back to the hotel now," said Ella. "Can you help me up? My foot . . ."

Lucas stood up. He gave Ella his hand. He only touched her hand, but his whole body felt it.

"Thanks," she said. "I don't want to make my foot worse."

"I'll . . . I'll walk back with you."

They said good night at the door of the hotel.

Lucas walked back onto the beach. He looked up at the moon. Then he pulled off his shirt and trousers. He ran into the water and swam away from the land in a straight line.

Chapter 6

A walk in the sun

Lucas was cleaning the Surf School boards the next morning when Ella appeared.

"You work hard," she said, "in the restaurant, at the surf school . . ."

"I've got to pay for my surfing life," he said. "How's your foot this morning?"

"It's okay, thanks," she said. "Much better."

"Are you here for a lesson?" he asked.

"No, not today. I'm just taking a walk. Have you got time to walk up on the cliff?"

"Give me five minutes," said Lucas. "I'll follow you up."

He put the boards away and ran along the sandy track up the cliff. Ella hadn't gone far. They walked for a while without speaking. It was windy up on the cliff, and there was salt in the air. The sun kissed the sea and turned it silver.

"Ella," Lucas started.

"Lucas," she said. "Last night, I wasn't trying to start anything between us."

"But there is something between us," said Lucas. "When I held your hand last night, didn't you feel it?"

"No, well, yes, but I'm going out with Jerry. He's my boyfriend. My life is in London. It's not fair to you or him."

"Why did you wait for me last night, then?"

"I was embarrassed by my friends. I wanted to say sorry, that's all. I've got to get back."

She turned and walked quickly back down toward the beach. Lucas ran after her.

"Wait!" he called out. "Will I see you again?"

"I don't know, Lucas. We're leaving this afternoon. I don't know when we're coming back."

They were on the beach now.

"Ella, can I call you?"

"No, Lucas. I'm sorry if I gave you the wrong idea. I'll see you when I see you."

Lucas watched her as she walked back to the hotel.

Later that day, Lucas watched the sea from the town beach. It was beginning to move.

Then his phone rang.

"Lucas, how's things?" It was his dad.

"Okay, Dad, good to hear from you," he said.

"I really need you here, Lucas," he said. "Can't you come out for the summer? I'll pay for you."

"I don't know. I'd like to come, but . . ."

"What's keeping you there?"

"A girl."

"Does she like sun, sea, and boats? Bring her, too."

"She's not my girlfriend, Dad," Lucas said. "I can't just bring her."

"Lucas! Who can say no to a handsome boy like you?"

"Yeah, yeah. I'll think about it, Dad. When do you need me?"

"At the end of the month?"

"Okay. I'll call you."

The waves were bigger now. He took his best board and swam out. It was getting late, and there weren't many people in the water. The noise of the sea was loud in his ears. A long, perfect wave came toward him. He stood up and flew along. His board became part of his body. He went back for wave after wave. People walking on the beach stopped to watch him.

It was nearly dark when he walked back up the sand. As he put his board away, he looked at a picture on the wall. It was one of Hawaii's biggest waves—"Jaws" they called it. The waves here were good, but they were nothing like the waves there.

"You want to be a real surfer," he said to himself, "then you've got to surf 'Jaws.'"

He called his dad.

"Give me a month, Dad, then get me a plane ticket," he said. "I'm on my way."

Chapter 7

The competition

Three weeks later, Lucas arrived for the surfing competition at the town beach. The car park was full, and he left his car on the road outside. The beach was full, too. He often won these local competitions and he really needed the money now.

Lucas joined the local boys near the water and watched the surfing. One of their friends did some amazing moves. They all cheered from the beach. When he came in, his name went up on the board in first position. Then it was Lucas's turn. He walked down to the water through groups of people. He was planning some difficult moves.

And then there she was. His heart jumped. She was more beautiful than he remembered.

"Ella," he said. "You've come back."

"Jerry and I . . ." she said. "It's over. I'm going to tell him tonight."

Lucas heard his name and competition number over the speakers.

"Does that mean . . . ?" he started to say, but Ella stepped back.

"Go on!" she said. "It's your turn. Good luck!"

He swam out and began to feel the sea. The first wave went past.

The second wave was good. He felt the power and timed his ride well. He reached the highest point of the wave and did some great moves. His friends cheered.

His next ride wasn't so good. And now there wasn't much time left; each surfer only had ten minutes. He picked up his last wave beautifully. But suddenly he thought about Ella, and nearly fell off the board.

"Oooh!" He heard the people on the beach.

He quickly got into a good position again. He finished the ride well.

"I won't win now," he thought.

He jumped off his board and pulled it out of the water. Lucas looked at the competition board. His number was in first position.

The last surfer in the competition walked past him on his way to the sea. It was Jerry.

"What went wrong?" he said to Lucas.

Lucas didn't reply, but looked for Ella. She was with her friends. When she saw him, she came to meet him.

"The last three weeks felt like three years," he said. "I've really missed you."

"The others went down to the north of Spain," she said. "The surf down there was amazing—near Bilbao, I think."

"What about you?" he said.

"I was working," she said. "I need the money to pay for my studies. And I was thinking . . ."

"Are you really finishing with Jerry?" asked Lucas. "Does that mean . . . ?"

Suddenly people on the beach were cheering. Lucas and Ella turned to watch. Jerry's first ride was great. His second wave was better. He surfed two more, and then his time was up.

Jerry came out of the sea with a very large smile on his face. The winners' names went up on the board. Jerry was first, Lucas was second. Lucas turned back to Ella.

"Does that mean . . . ?" he started to ask again.

Ella spoke quickly into his ear. "Let's meet tomorrow and talk. I must speak to Jerry first."

She went over to her friends. Suddenly Jerry was there next to Lucas.

"City boys always win in the end," he said. And then he stopped smiling. "Ella likes winners. Did you know that? Now who won the competition? Oh yes . . . I won it."

"Did you?" asked Lucas, and he walked away. He put his board in the Surf School and went to his car. Jerry's red sports car was right behind it.

He put his orange bag on the back seat of his car, but then he decided to walk home. He wanted time to think. He went up on the cliff behind the beach and looked down. He saw Jerry and Ella. They were arguing. Ella turned and walked over to her girlfriends. Jerry went the other way, toward his car. Lucas watched him for a moment and then turned for home.

Chapter 8

The fishing knife

The Tube restaurant was hot and noisy. All the tables were full. Lucas saw them before they saw him.

"Don't give them one of my tables," he said to the manager.

"Okay, Lucas," said George, the manager. "But I don't want trouble. I don't like it."

"Thanks," said Lucas, and he went into the kitchen.

He didn't go near their table all evening. Jerry called him three or four times, but one of the other waiters went over.

"Take ten minutes' break, Lucas," said the manager at half past eleven.

Lucas went through the kitchen and into the car park. There was a seat near the door, and he sat down. He enjoyed the cool air and the smell of the sea. Twenty minutes later, when he was back in the kitchen, there were shouts from the restaurant.

"Jerry," he heard one of Jerry's friends call. "Someone's cut the tires on your car."

"What! I'm calling the police!" Jerry was shouting at the manager. Then he saw Lucas. "It was him," he said.

"What's going on?" said Lucas.

"Call the police and come outside," shouted Jerry.

Everyone went out to the car park. They looked at Jerry's car.

"Look!" shouted Jerry. "He cut my tires with his knife."

"How do you know it was him? Did you see him?" asked Ella. She was afraid.

"I'm sure it was him. He's jealous of me. He wants my car, my life . . ." said Jerry, ". . . and my girl."

"What?" said the manager. "Lucas is a good boy. He doesn't do things like this. Never!"

The blue lights of a police car appeared.

"That guy," Jerry told the police officer. "He came out here while we were eating. He cut the tires on my car."

"Did you see this happen?" asked the police officer.

"No, I was inside. But he and his friends don't like us," said Jerry. "They want us to leave town."

The police officer turned to Lucas.

"I was working in the restaurant all evening," said Lucas. "I didn't do this."

The police officer turned to the manager.

"That's right . . . but . . . well . . . Lucas came out here for ten minutes for his break."

Everyone was surprised.

"But he's a good boy," the manager said. "He doesn't make trouble."

The police officer turned back to Lucas. "What did you do in your break?" she asked.

"I sat on the seat over there, outside the kitchen."

"Is your car in the car park?"

"Yeah, it's over there," said Lucas.

"I'll take a look inside."

She didn't find anything.

"What about his coat or his bag?" asked Jerry's friend.

The manager took them to the kitchen. Lucas's orange sports bag was on the floor. The police officer opened it—there was the knife that Lucas used when he went fishing.

"That's your knife," said the manager. "I know your knife, Lucas! Did you do this?"

"No, of course not!" said Lucas.

The police officer took Lucas to the police car. He passed Ella.

"I didn't do it," he said. "You must believe me."

Ella turned away.

Chapter 9

Titan

"I'm sorry, Lucas," said the restaurant manager the next morning. "I don't believe him—that crazy guy. But I don't want trouble in my restaurant. Some people don't like trouble—they don't come anymore. Some people, they like trouble—they come. Trouble brings more trouble. Lucas, it's business. You're a nice boy. I'm sorry."

Lucas got into his car and drove to Karrek Beach.

"Great!" thought Lucas. "No girl. No job. No money. And I'm in trouble with the police. How did all that happen? I can't wait to get on that plane to Maui."

The sky was dark gray. There were no people on Karrek Beach, and the waves were very high. They were much higher than normal. Lucas picked up a perfect wave. The sound and the power of the sea filled his head and his heart. He shouted above the angry waves.

The waves got bigger. A strong wind was coming across the sea. Seabirds went round and round in the air over the beach.

"Whoah!" said Lucas. A mountain of water was coming. It was a Titan. Lucas decided not to try it. He came out of the water, picked up his phone, and texted his friends, "Titans on Karrek!"

His friends soon arrived, but they didn't want to try surfing. They stayed safe on the beach and watched the sea. Then a red car appeared at the top of the cliff.

"I don't believe it!" shouted Lucas.

Jerry was with two of his friends.

"I got my car back," said Jerry. "I had to buy four new tires."

"Are you happy now?" asked Lucas. "I lost my job because of you. It wasn't me and you know that."

"Sorry, but we all know it was you," said Jerry. "It was your knife and it was in your bag. End of story."

"Why are you here?" said Lucas.

"We heard about the Titans," smiled Jerry. "Your friends say only you can surf them. Let's see about that. Are you ready? You against me. How about it?"

He looked at his friends and smiled.

"It's dangerous, Jerry. You can break your back out there," warned Lucas.

"OK. You stay on the beach and watch me."

Jerry swam out to the waves, and Lucas watched.

"He's crazy," said Lucas. "This is crazy."

Then he picked up his board and followed Jerry. The waves were really big now. Lucas was afraid. Jerry got into a good position. He shouted something at Lucas, but Lucas could only hear the sea. Lucas moved away from Jerry.

And there was a Titan. A blue-black mountain of water was moving toward them. The two young men got up on their boards. Jerry went first. Jerry screamed and laughed when he felt the power of the water. But as the wave came toward the beach, there was no time to turn. Jerry's board ran into the cliff at the side. He hit his head on the rocks, and the sea pulled him under. Lucas was twenty seconds behind him on the next wave. He jumped off his board. The sea pulled him down too. As the wave broke onto the beach,

Lucas swam up for air. He looked around for Jerry. He saw the board but no Jerry. He shouted his name. He looked across the water; another wave was coming in. It was smaller but he was in a dangerous place. Then he saw Jerry. He swam fast to him. He took him in his arms as the wave pushed them down again. He held him. When they came back up, Lucas swam hard for the beach.

"Lucas! Jerry!" Ella was running down the beach.

Everyone on the beach helped to carry Jerry. They put him down.

Lucas put his mouth to Jerry's mouth. Nothing. He tried again, and one of Jerry's friends pushed on his heart. Suddenly water came out of Jerry's mouth.

"Call for help," shouted Lucas.

Ella was already on the phone.

Chapter 10

Hawaii

When Lucas arrived at the hospital, Ella was in the waiting room. She ran toward him and took his hands.

"He's going to be fine," she said. "Lucas, you saved him. And he told me everything. He was the one that cut the tires on his car."

"I know," said Lucas. "How did he get my knife?"

"After the competition, Jerry and I argued about you on the beach. Your car was parked in front of his. He took the knife from your car then. He was so angry. He planned it all because he didn't want to lose me. I'm sorry, Lucas."

"Why?"

"I'm sorry because I believed him. About the tires."

"Why did you come back, then? Why were you at the beach?"

"Because I didn't want to believe him. I wanted to be wrong. I followed him to Karrek Beach. I wanted to see for myself."

They went outside.

"I finished with Jerry yesterday, after the competition," said Ella.

"Yes!" cried Lucas and he danced around the car park. Ella laughed.

"Come with me to Hawaii for the summer," Lucas said. "I'm going to work for my dad. There'll be a job for you, too. And we can do some real surfing . . ."

"I don't know, Lucas. I don't know you very well. You don't know me."

"You can get to know me in Hawaii," he said. "We can get to know each other."

She smiled.

"You said you wanted to be here," she said.

"I want to be with you," said Lucas.

She thought for a moment.

"Give your dad a call then," she said. "It sounds perfect!"

"Come here," said Lucas, and he kissed her.

Review: Chapters 1–5

A. Match the characters in the story with their descriptions. Use the names in the box.

Lucas	Ella	Jerry
Max	Lucas's dad	

Which of these characters. . .

1. brings the city boys to the secret beach? _____

2. breaks his surfboard on Karrek Beach? _____

3. drives an old blue car? _____

4. surfed for the first time a few weeks ago? _____

5. grew up by the sea? _____

6. is working in Hawaii? _____

7. shares a house with lots of students? _____

B. Are these statements about city boys or local boys? Write C or L next to each sentence.

1. They're studying law at university. _____

2. They sometimes go to France or Spain for the weekend to surf. _____

3. They surf every day at Karrek Beach. _____

4. They drive fast cars with powerful engines. _____

5. They don't have much money. _____

C. Circle the correct word or phrase in italics to complete each sentence.

1. Karrek Beach is *an easy / a difficult* place to surf.

2. Lucas *is / isn't* interested in Ella the first time he sees her.

3. Max takes the city boys to the secret beach because they *can't find it / pay him.*

4. Ella's friends are all *good surfers / beginners* like her.

5. *Dancing / Swimming* is one of Ella's hobbies.

6. Lucas *asks / doesn't ask* Ella on a date after the lesson.

7. Lucas *starts / stops* a fight between Jerry and one of the local boys.

8. *Lucas's / Ella's friends* help her when she falls at the bottom of the cliff.

9. Lucas's car breaks down because *it's very old / Jerry drives into the back of him.*

10. Jerry sends his steak back because *it's badly cooked / he wants to embarrass Lucas.*

D. What do you think? Answer each question.

1. Why does Jerry act so badly when Lucas is there?

   _____

2. Which life would you prefer? Why?

   a. giving surfing lessons in a town by the sea

   b. studying law in a capital city

E. Match the first and last parts of each sentence.

1. Karrek Beach   a. is next month.

2. Surfing   b. is a restaurant.

3. A "Titan"   c. is a local secret.

4. The Tube   d. is like dancing on the waves.

5. The surfing competition   e. is a very big wave.

F. Choose the best answer for each question.

1. When Lucas surfs, he feels

    a. afraid of the sea.

    b. like part of the sea.

    c. bored with his life.

2. Jerry

    a. is very sure of himself.

    b. doesn't like trouble.

    c. respects other people.

3. Ella

    a. is just like Jerry.

    b. comes from a very rich family.

    c. is a normal girl.

4. The local boys

    a. want to share Karrek Beach with the city boys.

    b. want to keep Karrek Beach for themselves.

    c. only come to the beach at weekends.

G. Which of these things do you think will happen in the second part of the story? Check (✔) the things you think will happen.

_____ Jerry and Lucas will fight.

_____ Ella will run away with Lucas.

_____ Jerry will ask Ella to marry him.

_____ Jerry will win the surfing competition.

_____ Lucas will win the surfing competition.

_____ (your idea)

Review: Chapters 6–10

A. Read each statement and circle whether it is true (T) or false (F).

1. On the cliff walk, Ella says she has no feelings for Lucas. T / F

2. Lucas's dad wants Lucas to work for him over the summer. T / F

3. Lucas decides to go to Hawaii. T / F

4. Lucas doesn't see Ella for three weeks before the competition. T / F

5. Ella and her friends have been down to the north of Spain. T / F

6. Jerry and Ella have an argument on the beach. T / F

7. The police officer finds Lucas's fishing knife in his car. T / F

8. Lucas loses his job because the manager doesn't like him. T / F

9. Lucas saves Jerry's life. T / F

B. Answer each question.

1. Why does Lucas decide to go to Hawaii? _____

2. Why does Lucas want to win the surfing competition?

3. Why does Lucas suddenly make a mistake in the surfing competition?

4. When does Lucas have time to cut Jerry's tires?

5. Why does Lucas think Jerry is crazy to surf a Titan?

C. How important are these things in Lucas's life? Put them in order from 1 to 5, with 1 being the most important and 5 the least.

_____ a. surfing

_____ b. Ella

_____ c. money

_____ d. a good job

_____ e. his family

D. Look at each statement from the story and answer the questions.

1. "It's our beach doctor." (page 22)

   a. Who says it?

   b. Who is he talking about?

   c. Is he being friendly or unfriendly?

2. "Why don't you come down and spend a weekend with me?" (page 25)

   a. Who says it?

   b. Who is he asking?

   c. What answer does he get?

3. "I'm sorry if I gave you the wrong idea." (page 28)

   a. Who says it?

   b. Who is she speaking to?

   c. What was the "wrong idea"?

4. "It's over. I'm going to tell him tonight." (page 31)

    a. Who says it?

    b. Who is "him" in the sentence?

    c. What's "over"?

5. "I didn't do it. You must believe me." (page 38)

    a. Who says it?

    b. Who is he speaking to?

    c. What didn't he do?

6. "Are you ready? You against me. How about it?" (page 40)

    a. Who says it?

    b. Who's he speaking to?

    c. What does he want to do?

E. Number these events in the order they happened (1 to 6).

    a. Jerry parks his car behind Lucas's car at the surfing competition. _____

    b. Lucas takes his break outside and then goes back to the kitchen. _____

    c. Jerry's friend finds the cut tires. _____

    d. Jerry sees Lucas's fishing knife and orange bag on the secret beach. _____

    e. Jerry takes the knife from Lucas's car after the competition. _____

    f. Jerry goes into the car park and cuts his car tires. _____

F. Explain why each of these things is important in the story.

    a. an overcooked steak

    b. a picture of "Jaws"

    c. an orange sports bag

G. What about you? Answer each question.

Have you ever been surfing?

What exciting sports would you like to try?

What's the most dangerous thing you've ever done?

Answer Key

Chapters 1–5

A:

1. Max **2.** Jerry **3.** Lucas **4.** Ella **5.** Lucas **6.** Lucas's dad **7.** Ella

B:

1. C; **2.** C; **3.** L; **4.** C; **5.** L

C:

1. a difficult
2. is
3. pay him
4. good surfers
5. Dancing
6. doesn't ask
7. stops
8. Ella's friends
9. it's very old
10. he wants to embarrass Lucas

D:

1. (Sample answer) Jerry wants to be the best at everything. He thinks Lucas may be a better surfer than he. Perhaps he's better looking, too.
2. Answers will vary.

E:

1. c; **2.** d; **3.** e; **4.** b; **5.** a

F:

1. b; **2.** a; **3.** c; **4.** b

G:

Answers will vary.

Chapters 6–10

A:

1. F; **2.** T; **3.** T; **4.** T; **5.** F; **6.** T; **7.** F; **8.** F; **9.** T

B: (Sample answers)

1. because Ella tells him she doesn't want to have a relationship with him and/or because he wants to surf "Jaws"

2. because he needs the prize money

3. because he thinks about Ella and not the wave

4. during his break

5. because it's dangerous

C: Answers will vary.

D:

1. a. Jerry	b. Lucas	c. unfriendly
2. a. Lucas	b. Ella	c. no answer
3 a. Ella	b. Lucas	c. that she wanted to have a relationship with him.
4. a. Ella	b. Jerry	c. their relationship
5. a. Lucas	b. Ella	c. cut Jerry's tires
6. a. Jerry	b. Lucas	c. surf a Titan

E:

In order: d, a, e, f, b, c

F:

(Sample answers) Ella spends time with Lucas because of the overcooked steak. Lucas decides to go to Hawaii when he sees the picture of "Jaws." Jerry knows that Lucas keeps a knife in his orange sports bag.

G:

Answers will vary.

Background Reading:
Spotlight on ... *Cornwall*

A. Read the information about Cornwall and answer the questions below.

Did you know Cornwall is part of England but it has its own language? Five hundred years ago, most people in Cornwall spoke Cornish. Today only a few hundred people can speak it fluently. But the language is coming back to life. If you visit Cornwall today, you see signs in Cornish as well as English. The Cornish word for Cornwall is "Kernow."

1. Do people speak any old languages where you live?

2. Is it important to keep old languages alive?

B. Read about one of Cornwall's old stories and answer the questions below.

Cornwall is famous for its old stories. King Arthur and the Knights of the Round Table fought and died here. People say that giants[1] and witches[2] once lived here. Unhappy lovers, like Tristan and Isolde, broke their hearts here. Read about what happened to one man on Bodmin Moor in Cornwall long ago.

The year was 1100. Robert, Earl of Moreton, was a good friend of William Rufus, King of England. Robert often rode his horse on Bodmin Moor in Cornwall. The Moor is a wild and open place. One day he was riding alone. He saw a large black animal. It came closer. The animal carried a man's body on its back. The body was black and wore no clothes. There was an arrow[3] through the man's heart. The animal spoke to Robert. "I am taking your king to the next world," it said. And then the animal and the body were gone.

At that hour, on that day, King William Rufus was killed by an arrow many miles away.

WILLIAM II.

1. What's your favorite old story from your country?

2. Do you ever believe stories like this?

C. Read the passage and answer the questions below.

Cornwall is long and narrow with the sea all around. It has 476 kilometres (296 miles) of cliffs and beaches. The Cornish people look to the sea for work. Today there are jobs at the surfing beaches. Lots of people come to Cornwall on holiday. But once upon a time there were wreckers.[4] Read this part of a letter from 1710.

"The Russian ship *Flora* was on its way to the Baltic Sea with wine and oranges. There was a terrible storm and the ship hit the rocks. It came onto the beach at Praa Sands. The local wreckers ran all over the ship. They stole everything, even the clothes from the Russian seamen. By the time the local officers arrived, the *Flora* was in pieces and nothing was left."

1. The ship *Flora* hit the rocks

    a. because of the storm.

    b. because of the wreckers.

2. Today Cornish people have jobs in

    a. tourism.

    b. wrecking.

[1]**giant:** a very large and tall person from old stories

[2]**witch:** a woman who can do magic

[3]**arrow:** a long thin piece of wood with a point at one end; in the past, it was used for fighting

[4]**wrecker:** a person who takes things from a ship that has hit the rocks

Background Reading:
Spotlight on ... *Surfing*

A. Read what surfer Jim Moore says about surfing the UK's biggest wave. Then answer the question below.

"I waited days for the right wave. Finally, there it was. Thirty feet (ten meters) of water came over the Cribbar Reef off Newquay in Cornwall. No one else was out there. I got some good rides and some good beatings. The waves push you down very deep. It can take a long time to come back up. I've been to Hawaii and Fiji to ride big surf. But there are always lots of people there. Here, you can surf big waves on your own."

How is the Cribbar different from big waves in Hawaii and Fiji?

B. Read about the world's biggest wave and answer the question below.

The world's biggest wave can be 21 meters (70 feet) high. It travels at 48 kilometers per hour (30 mph) and breaks onto a rocky beach. It comes a few times a year on the north side of the island of Maui in Hawaii. The locals call it "Peahi." The world's surfers call it "Jaws." And only the world's best surfers can surf through its giant tubes. Surfers are taken out to "Jaws" by jetski or dropped in by helicopter. Surfing "Jaws" is "like jumping off a cliff," says top surfer Dave Kalama. "I like to just take a quick look at the wave, and go."

Would you be brave enough to try "Jaws"?

Glossary

bandage	(*n.*)	something you put around a cut on your skin to keep it clean
beat	(*v.*)	to throb or move regularly, as in a heartbeat
break down	(*v.*)	to stop working
cliff	(*n.*)	a high piece of land next to the sea
competition	(*n.*)	an event where two or more people do something to find out who is the best
jealous	(*adj.*)	an emotion you feel when you want something that someone else has
lawyer	(*n.*)	a person who practices the law
local	(*adj.*)	from the place where you live
respect	(*n.*)	showing that you think highly of someone because they know a lot or can do something really well
rock	(*n.*)	a hard piece of earth
sand	(*n.*)	Beaches are made of sand. (*adj.*) sandy
scream	(*v.*)	to make a loud noise suddenly because you are afraid or excited
secret	(*n. & adj.*)	something not many people know about
surf	(*n.*)	to stand on a board and ride a wave
tire	(*n.*)	a round and black piece of rubber; a car moves on these
trouble	(*n.*)	a problem between people, including arguing and fighting
wave	(*n.*)	a line of high water that moves across the sea

NOTES